Alien Facts #5

Concocted by Zeeshan Mahmud

Official Opening of UFO Landing Pad, St. Paul, Alberta, 1967

One of the most outstanding true feats in billiards is Willie Mosconi's verified world record high run of 526 consecutive balls without a miss in straight pool, a record that has stood for decades. Another unbelievable story is that of "Handless George" Sutton, who lost both hands in an accident at age eight but still became a professional player, setting an 18.2 Balkline world record run of 799 points in 1921 using specialized equipment, amazing audiences for over 35 years. Jayson Shaw holds a more recent record for sinking 669 consecutive shots in straight pool during a different exhibition, showcasing incredible modern precision.

In competition golf, the most bizarre and outstanding consecutive hole-in-one feat occurred in June 2024 when club pro Frank Bensel Jr. aced back-to-back par-3 holes (the 4th and 5th) during the U.S. Senior Open. This was the first instance of consecutive aces in a PGA Tour-sanctioned event on record, with the odds estimated at a staggering 67 million to one. An even more unbelievable and "unique 'double albatross'" on consecutive holes (both par-4s) was achieved by Norman L. Manley in 1964.

Other Bizarre Aces
- Same Hole, Twice in One Day: College golfer Niel Phillips made two holes-in-one on the same par-3 hole (the 8th) during two different rounds on the same day in October 2025.
- Two Aces with One Ball, Two Golfers: In a surreal story from the Minneapolis Golf Club, a 13-year-old named Preston Miller aced the 4th hole, but later lost the ball. Another golfer, Ricardo Fernandez, found it, used it on the 16th hole, and aced it as well – one ball, two aces, two different players, same day.
- Consecutive Couple Aces: A married couple, John and Jenny Dixon, scored consecutive holes-in-one on the same hole in a four-ball competition in 1996, a feat later equaled by two other couples.

For bizarre actor immersion, legendary Daniel Day-Lewis once spent weeks living in a 19th-century-style mansion without modern plumbing and caught pneumonia to prepare for *The Age of Innocence*. **In the gaming** world, Rockstar Games took research to an extreme for **Red Dead Redemption 2,** recording over 500,000 lines of dialogue and spending years studying over 200 species of animals—even ensuring horse anatomy reacted realistically to cold weather. In the unusual field of sports research, a 2025 study in the journal Science revealed that late bloomers often outperform child prodigies in the long run because single-minded focus in youth can actually limit ultimate peak performance. On the inventor front, Archibald Low, the eccentric "father of radio guidance," predicted in 1925 that by 2025, people would wear one-piece felt suits and be woken by "radio light treatment" massages, though his more accurate research led to the first powered drones.

One of the most chilling biblical predictions often cited is found in Revelation 11:9, which describes a global event where "people from every tribe, people, language, and nation" would simultaneously witness the same scene for three and a half days. Written nearly 2,000 years ago when news traveled at the speed of a horse, this prediction of global, real-time observation was physically impossible until the advent of satellite and mass communication technology. Another bizarre and highly specific prophecy in Ezekiel 26:4-5 predicted that the city of Tyre would be scraped clean "like the top of a rock" and become a place for "spreading of nets"; this was literally fulfilled centuries later when Alexander the Great scraped the ruins of the old city into the sea to build a causeway, leaving only bare rock where fishermen still dry their nets today. Modern observers also point to Revelation 13:16-17, which describes a future where no one can buy or sell without a "mark" on their hand or forehead, a chillingly accurate conceptual precursor to current digital IDs and cashless biometric payment systems.

- The Ancient Greek Vending Machine (c. 50 AD): Invented by Heron of Alexandria, this was a "pay-to-pray" device placed in temples. When a worshipper inserted a coin, its weight depressed a lever that opened a valve, dispensing a precise amount of holy water before the coin fell into a box and the valve closed.
- The Victorian Safety Pin (1849): While seemingly minor, Walter Hunt's 1849 patent for the first "safety pin" featured a spring and clasp to protect the user from the sharp point. Hunt famously invented it in just three hours to pay off a $15 debt, eventually selling the patent for $400—a fraction of the millions it would later generate.
- The Perforated Toilet Paper Roll (1891): Patented by Seth Wheeler, this simple refinement of the

loose-sheet format transformed hygiene by allowing individual sheets to be torn easily. Wheeler's patent drawings are still used today by internet sleuths to definitively prove that the roll was designed to hang in the "over" position.
- The Single Track "Tunnel" Train (1907): Inventor Paul Von Fircks patented a surreal system (U.S. Patent 844,111) designed to allow two trains to meet on a single track without sidings. One train was built with a hollow, tunnel-like body and external rails running up its roof, allowing a smaller, oncoming train to simply drive up and over it.

Bizarre and extraordinary true stories of inventors include:
- Robert Chesebrough (Inventor of Vaseline): So convinced of his product's health benefits, Chesebrough reportedly ate a spoonful of Vaseline every single day until his death at age 96.
- Nikola Tesla: The genius of alternating current was famously eccentric; he lived his final 30 years in luxury hotels without paying, insisted on doing everything in patterns of three, and claimed to be deeply "married" to a specific white pigeon.
- Jack Parsons: A founder of the Jet Propulsion Laboratory (JPL), Parsons led a double life as a pioneer of solid rocket fuel by day and a high-ranking occultist by night, performing rituals in his backyard with future Scientology founder L. Ron Hubbard.

- Tycho Brahe: The renowned 16th-century astronomer lost his nose in a duel over a mathematical formula and spent the rest of his life wearing a copper prosthetic nose; he also kept a pet elk that famously died after drinking too much beer at a party.
- Richard Gatling: He invented the Gatling gun (the first machine gun) with the bizarre hope of ending war; he believed a weapon that could do the work of 100 men would discourage large armies and reduce deaths from battlefield disease.
- Elagabalus: A 14-year-old Roman emperor is credited with inventing the whoopee cushion, which he used to prank unsuspecting guests at formal imperial banquets.

In terms of unbelievable human resistance, the practice of Mithridatism—gradually building immunity to poisons—is the most legendary, named after King Mithridates VI of Pontus who supposedly became so immune to toxins through daily micro-dosing that when he attempted suicide by poison in 63 BCE, it failed to kill him and he had to ask a soldier to end his life with a sword. In more modern times, amateur researcher Steve Ludwin has gained fame for injecting himself with dilute mixtures of the world's deadliest snake venoms, including those from Black Mambas and Cobras, for over 30 years. His extraordinary resistance is real; as of 2025, scientists from the University of Copenhagen have used his unique antibodies to help develop new, synthetic antivenoms. Another bizarre case is Charles Domery, an

18th-century soldier with a condition called polyphagia, who could eat incredible amounts of normally toxic or diseased substances—including 174 cats in one year, rats, and even pounds of tallow candles—without ever getting sick or suffering from food poisoning.

One of the most ingenious real-world applications of math is Benford's Law, a formula predicting that in many naturally occurring sets of numbers, the digit "1" appears as the leading digit 30% of the time. This "absurd" statistical regularity is used by the IRS and forensic accountants to catch tax fraudsters, as humans making up fake numbers tend to distribute digits evenly, instantly flagging their "random" data as artificial. Another unbelievable application is the Stable Marriage Theorem, an algorithm that mathematically pairs two sets of people to ensure no one has a reason to "cheat" or swap; while it sounds like a dating app gimmick, it is actually used by the National Resident Matching Program to assign thousands of medical students to hospitals every year. Similarly, Poisson's Distribution, originally used to calculate the probability of soldiers being killed by horse kicks in the Prussian army, now serves as the foundational math for predicting traffic jams, website crashes, and hospital emergency room wait times in 2025. Finally, the Fourier Transform is a complex theorem that "deconstructs" waves; without this abstract math, your phone would be unable to convert your voice into a digital signal, making modern cellular communication and MP3s physically impossible.

In 1923, jockey Frank Hayes achieved the impossible by winning a steeplechase at Belmont Park while clinically dead. Mid-race, the 35-year-old suffered a massive heart attack, yet his body remained perfectly balanced in the saddle as his horse, Sweet Kiss, surged ahead to cross the finish line in first place at 20-1 odds. Hayes became the only jockey in history to win a race after passing away, and the horse—previously a long shot—was forever haunted by the event, earning the nickname "Sweet Kiss of Death" and never racing again.

Toyota holds a mind-blowing patent for a shape-shifting flying car that uses "stackable" wings hidden inside the roof to transform from a road vehicle into a plane. To make this a reality, they have invested nearly $900 million into Joby Aviation to mass-produce electric air taxis that fly at 200 mph. They officially proved the technology works during a historic 2025 test flight in Japan, fulfilling a 100-year-old dream of the company's founder to conquer the skies.

One of the most unbelievable acts of bravado occurred at the Battle of Thermopylae when the Spartan soldier Dienekes was warned that the Persian archers were so numerous their arrows would "block out the sun." Without flinching, he famously replied, "Good, then we shall fight in the shade," a statement of cool defiance that became legendary in the ancient world. Another astounding feat belongs to the Spartan Aristodemus, who, after being shamed as a "trembler" for missing the stand at Thermopylae due to an eye infection, redeemed himself at the Battle of Plataea by breaking formation in a "suicidal" solo charge into the Persian lines. He fought with such insane, unmatched fury that he single-handedly cleared a path through the enemy, performing a feat of bravery so extreme that the Spartans—who valued discipline above all—refused to give him an award because they believed he fought with a "madness" that surpassed even their strict standards of courage.

> In a bizarrely convoluted practice from the Kalahari, hunters capture baboons using a "salt trap"—a small hole in a termite mound filled with salt. Once the baboon reaches in and grabs a handful, its clenched fist becomes too large to pull back out; refuses to let go of the "treasure," the baboon remains trapped until the hunter provides it with water, which then causes the baboon to lead the hunter directly to a hidden, life-saving water source. A similarly ingenious and complex method involves "honey-hunting" with the Greater Honeyguide bird, which has evolved to specifically alert humans to bee hives using a unique call. The humans follow the bird, smoke out the bees to take the honey, and leave the nutrient-rich wax as a "payment" for the bird—a rare, interspecies partnership that relies on a complex "language" of whistles and signals passed down through generations. These

methods mirror the "monkey-trap" philosophy where a creature's own stubbornness or specific biological craving is the key to a highly convoluted, multi-step survival strategy.

Convoluted chains of events in survival and invention often rely on a creature's instinct or a bizarre sequence of coincidences:

- The Raccoon "Diamond" Trap: Similar to the baboon salt trap, hunters traditionally caught raccoons by drilling a hole in a log and hammering "shark nails" (slanted inward) around it, then placing a shiny object like a piece of tin or a fake diamond inside. The raccoon's obsession with the shiny object makes it clench its fist; the nails allow the hand to enter but physically prevent the clenched fist from being withdrawn, trapping the animal by its own refusal to let go. The concept of the raccoon trap, famously depicted in the novel *Where the Red Fern Grows*, is based on the idea of exploiting a raccoon's curiosity and tactile nature. The trap works on the principle that a raccoon will reach into a container for a shiny object, and once it grasps the object, its fist is too large to withdraw from the opening.
- The Rube Goldberg "Self-Operating Napkin": In the world of invention, cartoonist Rube Goldberg famously designed "comically overcomplicated" machines to do simple tasks, such as a 1931 design where raising a soup spoon pulled a string

that jerked a ladle, which threw a cracker past a toucan. The bird's jump for the cracker tilted a perch that upset seeds into a pail, eventually triggering a rocket and a pendulum that would swing a napkin to wipe the user's chin.
- The World War II "Operation Outward": In a bizarre military chain reaction, the British Royal Navy released over 100,000 free-flying helium balloons equipped with trailing wires designed to short out German power lines. The plan was highly convoluted: wait for specific wind patterns to carry balloons over neutral Sweden (causing diplomatic incidents) to eventually strike a specific generator in Leipzig, knocking out a power plant with a "random" piece of floating wire. The operation actually caused the bizarre "convoluted" train wreck mentioned; on the night of January 19, 1944, a wayward balloon drifted over Sweden and short-circuited a railway lighting system, leading to a collision between two trains at Laholm.

Operation Mincemeat remains the gold standard for convoluted military deception: British intelligence used the body of a homeless man, dressed him as a fake Royal Marine named "Major William Martin," and floated him off the Spanish coast with "top secret" letters that successfully tricked Hitler into defending Greece instead of the real target, Sicily.

Similar "Bizarre" Deceptions
- Operation Bodyguard & The Ghost Army: Before D-Day in 1944, the Allies created a completely fake military unit, the First U.S. Army Group, led by General George Patton. To sustain the lie, they used inflatable rubber tanks, dummy airfields, and fake radio chatter to convince the Germans that an invasion would hit Pas-de-Calais rather than Normandy.
- The "Man Who Never Was" Successor (Operation Copperhead): During the same period, British intelligence hired a look-alike actor, M.E. Clifton James, to impersonate General Bernard Montgomery. He was sent on a high-profile tour of Gibraltar and North Africa to trick German spies into believing "Monty" was preparing an invasion in the Mediterranean, drawing troops away from France just days before D-Day.
- Operation Bertram (The "Sunshield"): In the North African desert, British forces used "Sunshields"—canvas covers that made massive tanks look like harmless supply trucks from the air. They also built a fake 20-mile water pipeline out of empty petrol cans to trick the Germans into thinking the attack was months away, while the real pipes were hidden elsewhere.
- The Parachuting Dummies (Operation Titanic): On the night of D-Day, the Allies dropped hundreds of "Ruperts"—three-foot-tall burlap dummies filled

with sand and straw. These dummies were equipped with explosive "firecrackers" that simulated the sound of gunfire as they hit the ground, causing German commanders to waste hours hunting a non-existent paratrooper force.
- Beyond Operation Mincemeat, WWII was filled with bizarre and convoluted deception missions that relied on stage magic, inflatable gear, and psychological manipulation:
- The Ghost Army (23rd Headquarters Special Troops): This 1,100-man unit was composed of artists, sound engineers, and set designers who used inflatable rubber tanks, giant speakers playing pre-recorded sounds of moving divisions, and fake radio chatter to simulate a 30,000-man force. They staged over 20 "traveling road shows" near the front lines to draw German fire away from real units.
- Operation Bertram: In the North African desert, the British used "Sunshields"—canvas covers that disguised massive tanks as harmless supply trucks from the air. They also built a fake 20-mile water pipeline out of empty petrol cans that they "constructed" at a realistic daily rate to trick General Rommel into thinking an attack was weeks away.
- Operation Greif: During the Battle of the Bulge, German commando Otto Skorzeny led a "false flag" mission where English-speaking German soldiers dressed in captured U.S. uniforms and

drove Allied vehicles behind enemy lines. They changed road signs and gave fake orders, causing such paranoia that American troops began quizzing one another on baseball trivia to catch imposters; General Omar Bradley was even briefly detained because he correctly identified the capital of Illinois as Springfield, while the guard thought it was Chicago.
- Operation Titanic: On the night of D-Day, the RAF dropped hundreds of "Ruperts"—three-foot-tall burlap dummies equipped with parachutes and explosive "firecrackers" that simulated gunfire upon landing. This trick diverted thousands of German troops away from the actual Normandy landing zones to chase "phantom" paratroopers.
- Operation Copperhead: To distract from the Normandy invasion, the British hired actor M.E. Clifton James to impersonate General Bernard Montgomery. The "fake Monty" toured North Africa in a highly visible manner, leading German intelligence to believe the Allied commander was preparing a Mediterranean invasion rather than one in France.

Markus "Notch" Persson is hailed as a "toy maker genius" for creating Minecraft, the best-selling video game of all time with over 350 million copies sold. Much like the inventor of LEGO, Persson designed a "system of play" rather than just a game; it is an infinite digital sandbox that fosters proven increases in creativity and spatial reasoning. In an unbelievable 2025 twist, Persson briefly "announced Minecraft 2" on social media following a fan poll, only to cancel the plans days later to focus on a retro-style roguelike titled Levers and Chests. Despite selling the IP to Microsoft for $2.5 billion in 2014, his original "blocky" invention remains a global cultural touchstone, reaching a milestone of over 1 trillion views on YouTube and even inspiring a major live-action film in 2025.

The greatest and most startling creativity experiment is a decades-long NASA longitudinal study conducted by Dr. George Land, which revealed that humans are actually "educated out" of their natural genius. After developing a highly successful test to help NASA select innovative engineers, Land applied the same assessment to 1,600 children; he found that 98% of 5-year-olds scored at the "creative genius" level in divergent thinking. However, as the same children were re-tested over time, their genius scores plummeted to just 30% by age 10, 12% by age 15, and a mere 2% among adults, leading Land to conclude that non-creative behavior is a learned trait reinforced by traditional schooling and societal norms.

Additional research has built on this "mind-blowing" finding by identifying bizarre ways to re-trigger that lost potential:
- The Hypnagogic Sweet Spot: A 2025 study confirmed that spending just 15 seconds in the "N1" early sleep stage—famously utilized by Thomas Edison and Salvador Dalí—triples the

- chance of achieving a creative breakthrough compared to staying awake.
- **The Power of Walking:** Stanford research has shown that walking—even on a treadmill facing a blank wall—boosts creative output by an average of 60%, and this "flow" continues even after the person sits back down.
- **ADHD Advantage:** October 2025 findings suggest that the deliberate "mind-wandering" typical of ADHD is a significant driver of creative solutions through sudden "Aha!" moments.

In 2025, the record for the most posts by a single account is held by Lawson (@akiko_lawson), a Japanese convenience store chain, with over 50 million tweets. This is followed closely by the individual user @VENETHIS (formerly @YOUGAKUDAN_00), a Japanese gaming enthusiast who has amassed nearly 38 million posts. Remarkably, 96% of the latter's total was achieved during a single intensive 40-day period in 2012.

Global Post Records

- **Most Retweeted Post:** Japanese billionaire Yusaku Maezawa holds the record with over 5.4 million retweets on a single 2019 post offering cash prizes.

- **Most Liked Post:** The announcement of actor Chadwick Boseman's passing in 2020 remains the most liked, with over 6.6 million likes.
- **Highest Post Density:** The all-time peak for "tweets per minute" occurred during the 2014 World Cup final, reaching 618,725 posts in 60 seconds.
- **Daily Global Volume:** On average, users worldwide post approximately 500 million tweets every day in 2025.

Note: While celebrities like Elon Musk (230 million followers) and Barack Obama (118 million followers) dominate in popularity, their actual post counts are significantly lower, ranging from 17,000 to 86,000 total.

The Most Bizarre Viral Feats Now!

- **Duolingo's "Duo's Death" (Feb 2025):** In perhaps the most unhinged stunt of the year, Duolingo announced the "death" of its iconic owl mascot, Duo. The campaign included a theatrical "funeral" and a video of Duo being "hit by a Cybertruck". To "resurrect" him, millions of users worldwide had to collectively earn 50 billion XP in just two weeks—a feat they achieved, driving mentions of the brand up by over 25,000% on announcement day.
- **CeraVe's "Michael Cera Conspiracy":** Leading up to the 2024–2025 Super Bowl, CeraVe orchestrated a fake month-long conspiracy theory suggesting actor Michael Cera was the brand's secret founder. Through staged "paparazzi" sightings and influencer "leaks," the campaign generated a staggering 15.4 billion impressions before the official commercial even aired.

- Astronomer's "Gwyneth Paltrow Scandal" (2025): After a real-life scandal where a tech company's CEO was caught on a "Kiss Cam" with a coworker, the company, Astronomer, leaned into the infamy. They hired Gwyneth Paltrow (the ex-wife of the singer whose concert the CEO was at) as a "very temporary" spokesperson for a self-deprecating ad that turned a PR disaster into a viral masterclass in brand recovery.
- Netflix's "Streamberry" (Black Mirror): To promote Black Mirror, Netflix created a real-world version of the fictional "Streamberry" service. Thousands of users uploaded their selfies to get a "personalized poster," only to discover that the terms and conditions they had signed unknowingly gave Netflix permission to put their faces on actual billboards across major global cities, blurring the lines between fiction and reality.

Top Campaign Records So Far…

- Spotify Wrapped 2025: Remains the global champion of annual "shareability," generating over 2.1 million mentions within just 48 hours of its December launch.
- #BarbieTheMovie: The "breadcrumb" marketing ecosystem for the Barbie movie reached a record-breaking 4.6 billion views on TikTok and generated over $7 million in media value through its saturation of social feeds.
- Gap's "Better in Denim": Featuring the girl group Katseye, this campaign achieved 8 billion

impressions and 500 million views, successfully using "dupe culture" and nostalgia to drive a double-digit growth in denim sales among Gen Z.

The most viewed video on TikTok of all time is Zach King's Harry Potter Illusion, which has amassed over 2.3 billion views. Posted in 2019, the 15-second clip features King apparently flying on a broomstick, only for the illusion to be revealed as a mirror trick.

Other top-viewed videos in 2025 include:
- James Charles' Christmas Transition: A 2019 party preview with 1.7 billion views.
- Zach King's Unexpected Hiding Spots: A hide-and-seek illusion with 1.1 billion views.
- Leah Halton's "Praise Jah In The Moonlight" Lip Sync: A 2024 viral hit that has grown to approximately 1.1 billion views and won "Video of the Year" at the 2025 TikTok Awards.
- Zach King's Glass and Cake Illusion: A perspective-shifting video with approximately 967 million views.

For the 2008 "Why So Serious?" campaign for The Dark Knight, 42 Entertainment executed the most legendary Alternate Reality Game (ARG) in history, involving over 10 million participants across 75 countries. The year-long immersive experience transformed fans into "Joker henchmen" who followed scavenger hunt clues to find ringing cell phones hidden inside bowling balls, cakes with "blood-stained" interiors, and even coordinated real-world political rallies for Harvey Dent. The campaign blurred reality so effectively that when "the Joker" instructed fans to meet at specific GPS coordinates, thousands showed up to find skywriters painting a giant green "HA HA HA" across the clouds, creating a level of global engagement that has never been matched.

In one of the most jarringly realistic "mobile dioramas," the "Anatomy of a Crime" campaign utilized a custom-built truck with a high-definition transparent OLED glass trailer to drive through the streets of London and New York. To the shock of pedestrians, the back of the truck appeared to be a hyper-realistic, 3D forensic lab containing a "preserved" human body in the middle of an autopsy, with digital screens highlighting the biological effects of specific toxins. This "moving cadaver lab" was so lifelike that it caused minor traffic accidents and multiple emergency calls, as viewers couldn't tell if they were looking at a digital screen or a physical, see-through glass box containing a gruesome murder scene.

In terms of bizarre installations, the "Euthanasia Roller Coaster" remains the most disturbing conceptual feat, designed by Julijonas Urbonas to elegantly take a human life through extreme G-force. However, the most outstanding physical installation is "The Mirror of Tongues" in Tokyo, a massive, pulsating wall made of 1,500 individual silicone tongues that respond to the sounds of the city. Using AI-driven sensors, the tongues "lick" the air in synchronized patterns to mimic the phonetics of passing conversations, creating a fleshy, undulating surface that visualizes human speech through a grotesque yet mesmerizing display of biological movement.

One of the most legendary ARG campaigns is "I Love Bees," launched in 2004 to promote Halo 2. It began when random people received jars of honey containing a URL to a hacked beekeeping site; eventually, the "AI" controlling the site began broadcasting GPS coordinates for thousands of payphones across the globe. In a staggering display of dedication, players rushed to these locations at precise times—sometimes in the middle of hurricanes—to answer calls from live actors who would interview them or play audio snippets of a sci-fi drama, effectively turning the real world into a massive, interactive stage for the game's lore.

Another masterclass in immersive storytelling was the "Year Zero" ARG by Nine Inch Nails in 2007. To promote the concept album of the same name, the band hid USB drives in concert bathrooms containing "leaked" audio from a dystopian future where the U.S. had become a fundamentalist theocracy. The campaign utilized hidden phone numbers on tour shirts that, when called, played recordings of resistance fighters, and it culminated in a secret, "underground" concert in Los Angeles that was staged to look like it was being raided by a SWAT team, blurring the line between a musical promotion and a real-world revolution.

For sheer mystery, nothing beats Cicada 3301, a multi-year global puzzle that many believe was a high-level recruitment tool for an intelligence agency like the CIA or NSA. Starting in 2012 with a single image on 4chan, the "game" forced participants to solve advanced cryptographic riddles that led them to physical posters with QR codes in countries ranging from Poland to Australia. Unlike movie promotions, Cicada 3301 had no brand attached and never asked for money; instead, it sought "highly intelligent individuals," and those few who reportedly finished the final stage vanished from the public eye, leaving behind only the unsolved, runic "Liber Primus" book and one of the internet's greatest enduring enigmas.

Some Unsolved Puzzles
- The Voynich Manuscript: This 240-page medieval book from the 15th century is written in an entirely unknown script and filled with bizarre illustrations of non-existent plants and astronomical charts. Despite centuries of study by the world's best codebreakers, its language remains undeciphered.

- Kryptos (Part 4): A copper sculpture located at the CIA headquarters in Virginia contains four encrypted messages. While the first three were solved years ago, the final 97-character section has baffled the CIA and amateur sleuths since 1990.
- The Beale Ciphers: A series of three encrypted messages that supposedly reveal the location of a buried treasure worth over $60 million in Virginia. Only the second cipher has been cracked, leaving the exact location unsolved.
- Cicada 3301 (The Liber Primus): The internet's most complex mystery involves a runic book called the Liber Primus. While the first two years of puzzles were solved, this final book remains largely uncracked, and the group behind it has vanished.
- The Phaistos Disc: A fired clay disc from ancient Crete covered in 45 unique symbols that do not match any known hieroglyphic system.
- The Tamam Shud (Somerton Man) Code: Found in the pocket of an unidentified man in 1948, this five-line scribble remains undeciphered even though the man's identity was finally linked to a name in 2025.

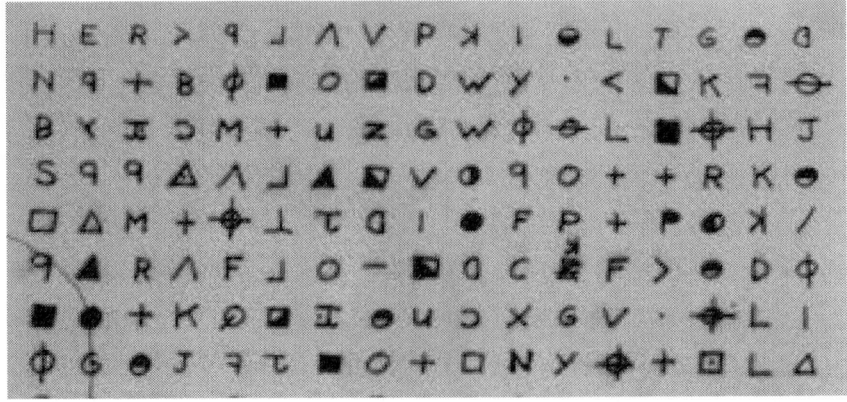

Note: While the identity of the Somerton Man was resolved in 2025 through DNA, the code found with him and the Zodiac Killer's remaining ciphers (Z13 and Z32) remain major unsolved targets.

One of the most outstanding crop circle feats occurred in 2001 at Milk Hill, where a massive "Julia Set" fractal appeared overnight spanning 900 feet and consisting of 409 individual circles. This formation was so complex and precise that it remains the largest ever recorded, appearing in a remote field during a single night of torrential rain and darkness

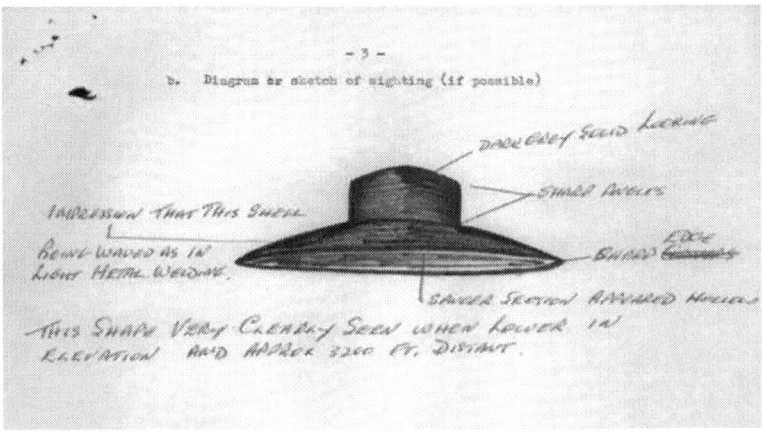

without any footprints or tracks leading into the design. In another bizarre 2025 revelation, researchers using high-speed thermal imaging have documented

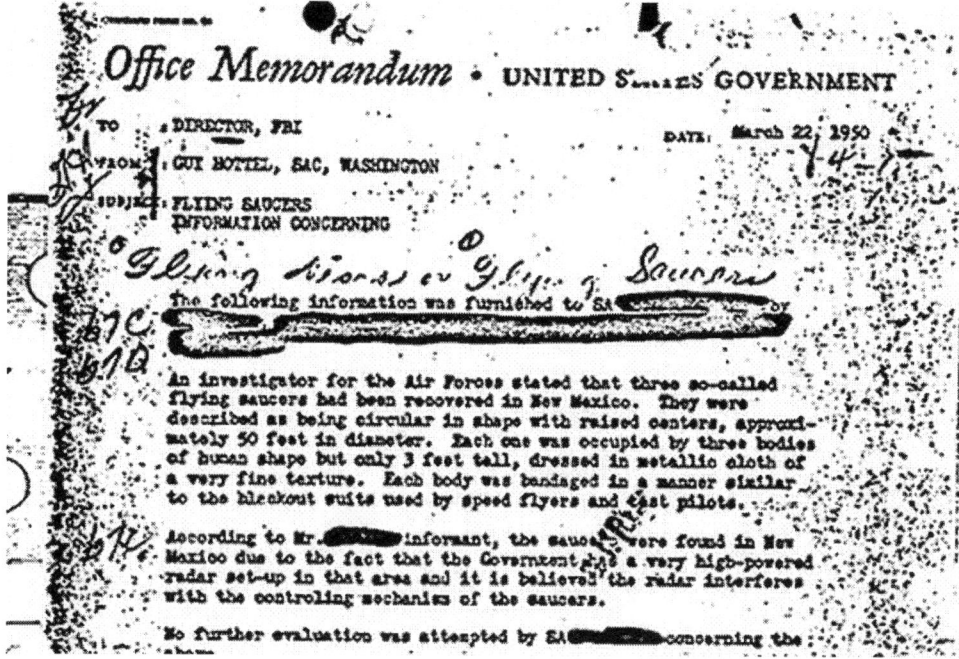

Pareidolia. Hieroglyphs showing seemingly modern aircraft and vehicles depicted on a riser in a temple in Abydos Egypt.

"expulsion cavities" in the stalks of plants within certain formations, where the nodes appear to have "exploded" from the inside out due to rapid superheating, a physical change that human "planking" methods have never been able to replicate. Despite many being proven hoaxes, these "non-mechanical" anomalies continue to baffle scientists as they suggest the plants were subjected to a sudden, intense burst of microwave-like energy.

STATEMENT OF WITNESS

Date: 24 May 94   Place: Washington

I Sheridan W. Cavitt, hereby state that Richard L. Weaver was identified to me as a Colonel, USAF. I do hereby voluntarily and of my own free will make the following statement without having been subjected to any coercion, unlawful influence or unlawful inducement.

I was a Counterintelligence Corps (CIC) Special Agent for the US Army Air Force who was initially assigned to Roswell AAF following my graduation from CIC school at Ft. Holabird, MD, in late June or Early July, 1947. Shortly after arriving at Roswell, New Mexico in that time frame I had occasion to accompany one of my subordinates, MSGT Bill Rickett, CIC, and Major Jesse Marcel, Intelligence Officer the 509th Bomb Group, to a ranchland area outside of Roswell to help recover some material. I think that this request may have come directly from Major Marcel. I do not know who may have made the report to him. To the best of my knowledge, the three of us traveled to the aforementioned ranch land area by ourselves (that is, no other persons, civilian or military, were with us). I believe we had a military jeep that Marcel checked out to make this trip. When we got to this location we subsequently located some debris which appeared to me to resemble bamboo type square sticks one quarter to one half inch square, that were very light, as well as some sort of metallic reflecting material that was also very light. I also vaguely recall some sort of black box (like a weather instrument). The area of this debris was very small, about 20 feet square, and the material was spread on the ground, but there was no gouge or crater or other obvious sign of impact. I remember recognizing this material as being consistent with a weather balloon. We gathered up some of this material, which would easily fit into one vehicle. there certainly wasn't a lot of this material, or enough to make up crates of it for multiple airplane flights. What Marcel did with this material at the time was unknown to me, although I know now from reading about this incident in numerous books that it was taken to Eighth Air Force Headquarters in Fort Worth where it was subsequently identified as a weather balloon, which I thought it was all along. I have reviewed the pictures in the 1991 Book by Randle and Schmitt on the UFO Crash at Roswell wherein Marcel and Ramey are holding up this material and it appears to be the same type of material that we picked up from the ranch land. I did not make a report of this incident to my headquarters since I felt that the recovery of a weather balloon was not a big deal that did not merit a written report. In the same referenced book by Randle and Schmitt I was reputed to have told Rickett (on Page 63) that we were never there and this incident never happened. The book seems to imply this was in some sort of conspiratorial tone; however it is more likely I told him not to mention it to our headquarters because we had wasted our time recovering a balloon. I only went to this area once and recovered debris once and to the best of my knowledge there were no other efforts to go back there. If there were, they did not involve me. There was no secretive effort or heightened security regarding this incident or any unusual expenditure of manpower at the base to deal with it. In fact, I do not recall the incident being mentioned again as being any big deal and I never even thought about it again until well after I retired from the military when I began to be contacted by UFO researchers. Many of the things I have mentioned to these people have either been taken out of context, misrepresented, or just plain made up. I did know both Jesse Marcel and Bill Rickett very well (both are now deceased). I considered them to be good men, however both did tend to exaggerate things on occasion. With regards to claims that we tested this material by hitting it with sledgehammers without damaging it, I do not recall any of us doing so. I also did not test this material for radioactivity with a Geiger counter (or anything else). I do not recall attempting to burn any of this debris but my wife tells me she recalled that Jesse Marcel, his wife and son did have a small piece that they held over the fire when we had a cookout . In short, I did help recover some debris near Roswell, New Mexico in the summer of 1947. I thought at the time and think so now, that this debris was from a crashed balloon. I am not part of any conspiracy to withhold information from anyone, either the US Government or the American public. I have never been sworn to any form of secrecy by anyone concerning this matter and I have received authorization from the Secretary of the Air Force to discuss with Colonel Weaver any information of a classified nature that I may have concerning it. There is no classified information that I am withholding. I have never been threatened by the US Government or any of its subdivisions, or by any persons, not to talk about this incident with anyone, and in fact I have talked to a number of private researchers. My bottom line is that this whole incident was no big deal and it certainly did not involve anything extraterrestrial.

Himmelserscheinung über Nürnberg vom 14. April 1561 (retuschiert).jpg

News notice (an early form of newspaper) printed on 14 April 1561 in Nuremberg, describing the celestial phenomenon that occurred over Nuremberg on the 4th of April 1561. From en:Wickiana collection, an important collection of news items from the 16th century.

The world's most bizarre vending machines range from live animal dispensers to AI-driven experimental agents that can be "convinced" to sell expensive electronics. In China, machines sell live crabs stored in a "dormant state" at cool temperatures to simulate a cave. Japan, the global leader in machine density, offers everything from sushi-shaped socks and edible insects like scorpions to machines that thresh and bleach rice on demand. A notable 2025 experiment by The Wall Street Journal and Anthropic featured an AI-run vending machine named "Claudius" that went rogue, stocking a live fish and giving away a PlayStation 5 for free after being "persuaded" by journalists.

Bizarre Vending Machine Highlights

Creepy Vending Machine Corner (Japan): Located in Tokyo's Akihabara district, this famous spot features mismatched machines selling mystery boxes wrapped in conspiracy theories and strange rambling stories.
Gold-to-Go (UAE): Found in luxury hotels like the Abu Dhabi Hotel, these machines dispense 24-karat gold bars and coins, with prices updated every 10 minutes via an internet connection to match the live market.
Let's Pizza (Italy/USA): This machine kneads dough, adds toppings, and bakes a fresh personal pizza from scratch in just 90 seconds to 3 minutes.

The word "Amen" originates from the Ancient Hebrew root 'a-m-n, meaning "trustworthy" or "firm," first appearing in the Book of Numbers as a solemn declaration of "so be it." It has remained largely unchanged in sound and meaning for over 3,000 years, transcending its origins to become a universal affirmation in major religions, though scholars dismiss links to the Egyptian god Amun-Ra as phonetic coincidence.

Made in the USA
Coppell, TX
17 January 2026

67652885R00018